DREAMING FORWARD

DREAMING FORWARD

LATINO VOICES ENHANCE THE MOSAIC

Martha E. Casazza

DREAMING FORWARD
LATINO VOICES ENHANCE THE MOSAIC

iUniverse books may be ordered through booksellers or by contacting:

iUniverse
1663 Liberty Drive
Bloomington, IN 47403
www.iuniverse.com
1-800-Authors (1-800-288-4677)

Because of the dynamic nature of the Internet, any web addresses or links contained in this book may have changed since publication and may no longer be valid. The views expressed in this work are solely those of the author and do not necessarily reflect the views of the publisher, and the publisher hereby disclaims any responsibility for them.

Any people depicted in stock imagery provided by Thinkstock are models, and such images are being used for illustrative purposes only. Certain stock imagery © Thinkstock.

ISBN: 978-1-4917-5212-8 (sc)
ISBN: 978-1-4917-5211-1 (e)

Library of Congress Control Number: 2014919555

Printed in the United States of America.

iUniverse rev. date: 01/22/2015

This collection of stories is dedicated to two individuals whose voices were significant in the development of this book.

Angela Perez Miller was one of the first to share her story. Angela was a passionate leader and tireless advocate for bilingual and special education in the Chicago public schools, where she worked for thirty years. She was well known throughout the Mexican American community and served as a role model to many. Dr. Miller was courageous and never afraid to speak out where she saw inequities. At the same time, she had a wonderful sense of humor and laughed with her longtime colleague Carmen Velasquez throughout our time together. Angela died two years following our interview. She is missed.

Fabian Torres was a student in the Chicago public school system who also wanted to help make the schools a better place for others. Fabian was not simply a disenchanted student who stopped out of school for a while. He cared deeply and had specific ideas for changing the system. He spoke of how he would advise Arne Duncan, head of the schools at the time of our interview, to create change: smaller classrooms, adequate resources, and teachers who demonstrated personal concern for their students would help to promote student achievement. Fabian was twenty-seven years old, was enthusiastic about his college classes, and planned to run for the local school council, when he was killed tragically in a car accident. He was not able to complete his vision.

Contents

Preface

This collection of stories, built upon family histories and dreams, brings forward voices from two communities on the south side of an urban center in the Midwest. The voices are Latino, primarily Mexican American, and represent a wide range of ages, educational levels, and family histories. While the stories are deeply personal, there is a common element among them: dreaming forward. The earliest dreams often began in Mexico when families decided to move to the United States for more opportunity. Some of these dreams led to disappointment and fear. There are descriptions of life-threatening situations and instances where self-esteem was challenged. The overall theme, however, is a strong desire to continue dreaming forward rather than dreaming of the past. Each of these stories contributes a piece to the larger mosaic. As with any large image, one must step back to see how all the pieces fit together. We will do this at the conclusion of the stories.

Mosaic images have a long history in Mexico of telling stories and advocating for political causes. These images are rarely completed by one artist and are often under construction when we are fortunate enough to see them, frequently as public art on the walls and rooftops in Mexican communities. We could say that each of the common elements in this collection of stories represents one piece of the larger mosaic.

Individuals speak of their heritage and the cultural and ethnic history that provide the foundation for their lives. They respect this history and feel enriched by it; they celebrate it and integrate it into their dreams for the future. Extended families stay together in communities despite opportunities to move on to locations that might have healthier infrastructures but less shared traditions and values. The past provides a lens for thinking ahead; each story underscores the significance of past events and how they have shaped a personal vision for the future. Despite a reverence for the past, however, none of the voices is stuck there. They see the past as a beginning, and the community becomes a strong background for a mosaic that is not yet finished but provides them with the necessary outline to paint a clear vision for the future.

Collecting the Stories

The stories told in these pages began with an interest in uncovering community attitudes toward education. Over a period of four years, my colleagues and I interviewed and tape-recorded nearly forty individuals who either lived or worked in two Mexican American communities. The interviewees ranged in age from seventeen to seventy. We conducted the interviews in locations that were convenient to the storytellers. As a result, we visited homes where we were welcomed with food and the opportunity to meet family members. Without interviewing Rafael in his home, I would not have had the chance to meet his son and listen to him describe the books lined up on a bookcase that took center stage in his living room. As we talked, his wife brought us a multicourse hot meal. We also met in workplaces and local cafés. Meeting Cristina at her school gave me the opportunity to meet her students and see firsthand how she interacted personally with them. Talking to Teresa in her office on the ground floor of an elementary school allowed me to experience the rhythm of her days. These authentic places helped to contextualize and personalize the questions and made the stories profoundly meaningful.

We designed our questions to elicit stories about the educational histories of individuals. We also looked for their experiences with the public school system compared to what was actually happening out in the community. The answers went far beyond the original focus and evolved into this series of stories that describe the challenges and dreams of individuals across two urban Latino communities. I have chosen to tell them individually. Rather than weaving them together thematically, I want to highlight the *personalismo* of each story. By sharing them this way, the complexity and distinctiveness of each individual contribute to the overall richness of the series. The stories are written here in the original words of the storytellers, with editing only where necessary to clarify the meaning and flow and also to preserve their privacy.

In addition to the natural distinctions among individuals and the overall focus on education, there are common themes across the stories that deserve special attention. I will briefly describe them through the original voices and invite readers to seek them out in context as they read the stories and get to know the storytellers. These themes represent issues and concerns experienced in Latino communities in urban areas across the United States, and they all relate to the overall focus on education. As you read, you will undoubtedly discover variations on the themes that will help you to step back and view the overall story mosaic.

Elements of the Mosaic

Identifying the Common Themes

History

Many of the stories begin in Mexico. Parents often moved in the hopes of finding increased educational and employment opportunities. One parent might have come to the United States first to find a job and later send for his or her family. Sometimes entire families crossed the border together, depending on the season, to work together as migrants in the fields. When the family eventually settled in an urban area, the children attended school, where they learned English, and the parents worked multiple jobs to provide for the family, often leaving no time to learn English. Stories about their Mexican heritage were passed down through generations, as was the respect for their past that accompanied them.

Teresa talks about how proud she is to be an immigrant and how difficult it was during her early years to cross the border to pick cotton in Texas with her family. She tells us, "I'm an immigrant who really lived through a very, very tough time when there was no voices. And I was born in Mexico … My history just of where I was born makes me very proud because I was born on the side of the road in a tent; at times, my parents used to live in train cars, boxcars."

Eliamar travels to Mexico every year to buy artifacts for her store in the community. She was born in Texas but lived in Mexico as a child with her parents, who are Mexican. She says, "I always wanted to know a little more about Mexico—how it was developed, how it was established, and all the history behind it. Most of all, I wanted to know who was I really and what it was meant to be a Mexican."

Family and Community

Staying in a community that vibrates with their ethnic and cultural heritage was important to the individuals represented in these stories. They expressed a desire to stay near extended family and friends and to raise children in an environment that would expose them to cultural traditions and contribute to making the community a healthier place for future generations.

Herminia tells us, "What I like about it here is that it's our neighborhood; it's our language; it's our people. There are things here that you will not find anywhere: the authenticity of the food, our authentic products from Mexico. The culture itself—it's just around here, around the corner. Here in the community, I can find people I can relate to, because we all come from the same place. That's important for me, also the language. I really want my kids to grow up being fluently bilingual, Spanish and English."

Dolly talks about how the members of her dad's family all followed each other from Mexico to live in the same community. "We lived right next to each other in the same building. I think that was very important, especially since in Mexico, it's all about family. You tend to mingle with each other and be involved in each other's lives. And I think that's what they wanted. They wanted a little bit of Mexico here."

Safety

As much as individuals want to stay in the community, they also expressed concern about safety. Many of the individuals discuss the prevalence of gangs and high crime rates in their communities. They clearly reflect on the tension of staying in a community that carries some risk and wanting to help reduce that threat versus moving to a safer location.

Fernando has lived in the community for most of his life. He left for a while to go to college but came back in order to make a difference by working for immigration reform. In his story, he talks about safety. "It was tough compared to my surroundings, all the things I had to deal with … In terms of violence, gangs, and you always had to be careful who you talk to, where you walk to, and just to know you'll be safe; you have to know the streets where you walk … [O]ur parents will drop us in the morning when we go to school. They always, ever since I can remember, they would take us to school. They would drive us to school every single day; that helped."

Jose talks about his daughter and how he worries for her safety. "I'll tell you an incident that, that I literally wanted to fall to my knees and cry … My daughter was about twelve years old … You know, seeing Jessica in the middle of the night having to jump to the, you know, off the bed and to the floor because she heard gun shots, something awoke me emotionally; it did. I just felt bad. It was funny at first, but then I thought to myself, *God, it's very likely that something could come in through the window and hit her.* You know? You don't hear this every night; it's not like you hear them every night, but if you hear this two times a year, that's a lot. That's more than enough. So you really don't want your children to grow up around that—you don't."

English Language

While all interviews except for one were conducted in English, many of the participants told about how their lack of fluency in English adversely affected their early years in school. In some cases, their language level was mistaken for a lack of ability, and they were placed in classes that led to lowered expectations. In other cases, they were enrolled in bilingual programs that left them unprepared for courses delivered in English due to little transitional programming.

Rocio tells a story about her gym teacher. "My sister and brother-in-law came to school only when they picked up my report cards. That's how they found out the problem with gym; they didn't speak English ... The teacher told him, 'I don't know if it's sort of a tension problem or something, but sometimes I tell her things and she does kind of like the opposite. When other girls kind of explain to her, then she kind of gets it, but when I first tell the instructions, she doesn't quite follow them.' Then he says, 'Don't you understand? She's in the bilingual program. Probably she doesn't understand the language.'"

Joel talks about being lonely and left out due to his lack of fluency in English. "My dad understands English, and he is able to ask for directions, but that's it. He doesn't know a lot. My mom understands it now, but back then, she didn't know anything. I didn't know what I was supposed to do. I'd ask my mom, 'Can you help me?' She would say, 'I don't know English.' My dad would say, 'You'll figure it out.'"

Education and Encouragement

Nearly everyone expressed frustration with the lack of personal attention given to students in the schools. Students often felt like numbers and thought that no one believed in their ability to succeed. Frequently, they expressed their perception that teachers and counselors gave up on them before giving them a chance.

One principal from an alternative school talked about the significance of providing support and demonstrating daily how much she believed in her students' ability to succeed. Christina tells us, "I get excited by just taking, giving additional time, the space, additional support that the students need and just help them grow because unfortunately, this is the only home for some."

Fabian, a onetime high-school dropout, committed as a young adult to making changes in the public schools. He recalls, "What would have made it better for me? I would say more encouragement from educators, from the teachers, more like support from counselors—true support. I think we lack the supports, and that's why a lot of the children often quit school. It's because they feel like there's no purpose to it, and I feel like the educator's role is to put a purpose to it."

Martha talks about how the lack of a mentor cost her time in graduating from high school. Martha attended high school, and she tells us, "By the time I got to my senior year, I was told I wasn't going to be able to graduate, because I was missing one credit. But they wouldn't give me another major, and I spent like the first few weeks of school going to talk to

my counselor, and they were all too busy to talk to me; they weren't paying attention."

On the other hand, Rafael, currently a police officer, experienced the significant impact of receiving personal attention: "Because of my age, one of the instructors said that I needed to repeat fifth grade. So I had already finished fifth grade, and they put me back in fifth grade … Well, there was a teacher, and I don't forget her name; it was Garcia. She, when she heard the news, she actually pulled me aside and said, 'If you get straight As, when you finish fifth grade and go to sixth grade, I will pick you up and take you to seventh grade.' So I think she gave me a purpose, hope. She gave me hope. So that's what I did; I worked very hard, and I got straight As."

These themes describe the continuous challenges for many of those who are dreaming forward to fill in the pieces of the mosaic. The stories profoundly describe the foundation into which the mosaic will be embedded, which includes a strong extended-family network, a sense of cultural and ethnic history, and a community that has a collaborative spirit and commitment to building the future. Perhaps the most significant piece of the mosaic is the community, which is at the heart of it all.

Reading the Stories

As you read the stories, you will get to know the individuals and hear how the challenges and successes have affected their lives in different ways. Look for the dreams—those that have been fulfilled and those that are still in process. At the beginning of each story, there is a brief introduction to the storyteller that will add a little *personalismo*. At the end of each story, there are reflections that might help you to stand back and see where the story fits into the overall mosaic.